HOW TO
MARKET YOUR
PRODUCT
ONLINE

DENISE C . MCBRIDE

Table of content

INTRODUCTION

Having a solid online presence is more pivotal than ever in the ultramodern digital age. Given that further and further implicit guests are using the internet to probe and buy goods and services, this is especially true for companies. Although it may be a grueling and dynamic field, online marketing is pivotal for companies of all kinds. You can develop and apply an effective internet marketing plan that will help you reach your target followership and expand your business by using the advice in this book. Recognising Your Target request Any effective marketing trouble starts with a thorough understanding of its target request.

With your product or service, who are you hoping to reach?

What problems and requirements do they have? After gaining a solid possess a thorough grasp of your intended followership, you can acclimate your marketing messaging meetly.

The following advice will help you comprehend your target followership

- To find out further about your sector and the individualities who are interested in it, conduct request exploration.
- To represent colorful target followership parts, use buyer personas.
- To find out what others are saying about your sector and your rivals, use social media harkening tools.

Formulating a Strategy for Content Marketing One of the stylish ways to draw in and keep interested guests is through *content marketing*. You may become an authority in your field and gain the confidence of your target followership by producing and propagating top- notch content.

You may produce a wide range of content formats, including blog entries, papers , podcasts, vids, and infographics.

Consider your target followership when deciding what kind of material to produce, and concentrate on subjects that will pique their interest and give useful information.

Search Engine Optimisation for Your Website ;The practice of perfecting your website to appear advanced in Search Engine Results Pages(SERPs) is known as Search Engine Optimisation, or SEO. You want your website to rank largely in Search engine results when prospective guests look for terms associated with your product or service. This will draw their attention to your website. You may employ a wide range of SEO strategies, including link structure, on- runner optimisation, and keyword exploration, to raise the standing of your website. Utilizing Social Media to Announce Your Goods Social media is a useful instrument. to announce your goods or services. It enables you to establish direct connections and connections with possible guests. Producing top- notch content that appeals to your target followership is pivotal when utilising social media for marketing. Responding to the queries and commentary of your followers is another way to interact with them. Using Sponsored Content to Announce Your Goods Using paid advertising can help you vend your goods or services more fleetly and reach a larger followership. Donated advertising platforms come in a variety of formats, including Google Advertisements, Amazon Advertisements, Facebook Advertisements, and LinkedIn Advertisements. Budget and target followership selection are pivotal factors to take into account when opting a paid advertising platform. Also, you have to duly plan your advertising strategies to make sure they work well.

Assessing the issues of Your Internet Marketing Conditioning It's critical to track the issues of your internet marketing juggernauts in order to determine what's and isn't effective. Over time, this will help you in enriching your marketing plan. You may cover a wide range of KPIs, including website business, leads produced, and deals. multitudinous results are available for tracking marketing issues, including HubSpot and Google Analytics.

For companies of all sizes, internet marketing is pivotal, but it can be a grueling and dynamic field. You may develop and put into practise an effective internet marketing plan that will help you in achieving your pretensions by using the advice in this book. reach your target request and expand your company. It's important to track your issues and maintain thickness in your web marketing sweats so you can determine what's and isn't working. You may use internet marketing to negotiate your business objects if you put in a little time and trouble.

Chapter 1

Having a solid online presence is more pivotal than ever in the ultramodern digital age.

This is particularly true for companies, as more and more prospective guests are using the internet to probe and buy goods and services.

For companies of all sizes, internet marketing is pivotal, but it can be a grueling and dynamic field. A good internet marketing plan may be created and enforced by clinging to the advice in this book. It'll enable you to expand your business and connect with your target request.

What makes internet marketing pivotal?
Online marketing is pivotal for organizations for several reasons. These are but a sprinkle

Expand your followership

With internet marketing, you may expand your followership to a worldwide followership. You aren't confined to those who live in your neighborhood.

Aim for your followership

Internet marketing enables you to direct your advertising dispatches towards particular demographics. This implies that you may more successfully communicate your asked clientele.

Value your issues

Compared to traditional marketing strategies, online marketing is more quantifiable. This implies that you can cover what's and isn't effective, allowing you to gradually enhance your sweats.

Inexpensive
Online marketing may be incredibly affordable, especially when varied with further conventional forms of advertising.

** Internet marketing types **

Online marketing comes in a lot of kinds. These are a sprinkle of the most typical The practice of perfecting your website to have it appear advanced in search engine results pages(SERPs) is known as **Search Engine optimisation**, or SEO.

Pay- per- click(PPC) advertising With PPC advertising, you may buy the top spot on search engine results pages(SERPs) and other websites for your announcements. material marketing is the process of producing and propagating worthwhile, timely, and coherent material in order to draw in and hold on to a specific followership and encourage economic consumer

Social media marketing:

Using social media platforms to engage with current and future consumers and advertise your products is known as **social media marketing or services**

Marketing via email: Email marketing is obtaining the email addresses of both current and prospective clients in order to send them marketing emails.

Businesses of all sizes may benefit from online marketing's potent tools, which can help them expand and connect with their target market. You may start online marketing and develop a winning online marketing plan by using the advice in this chapter.

Introduction to internet marketing**

Here are some pointers to help you get started if you're new to web marketing:

1. **Explain your objectives**:

What do you hope to accomplish with your internet marketing campaigns?

Which goals are you trying to achieve?

Lead generation, sales, or brand awareness?

Knowing your objectives can help you select the best marketing techniques and approaches.

2. Study your intended audience:

To whom are you attempting to direct your internet advertising?

What are their problems and needs?
You can develop marketing messaging that appeals to your target demographic if you have a thorough understanding of them.

3. Select appropriate marketing channels:

Not every marketing channel is made equally. Certain companies and product categories are more appropriate for some channels than for others. Find out which channels are most effective for your business by conducting some research.

4. Create high-quality content: Relevant material that appeals to your target audience is essential if you want to succeed with internet marketing. These materials can be podcasts, films, infographics, blog entries, or articles.

5.market your product: To ensure that people can locate your high-quality content, you must market it. Email marketing, social media, and your website are all good places to advertise your content.

6.Monitor your outcomes: It's critical to monitor the outcomes of your internet marketing initiatives so. that you are able to observe what is and is not functioning. Over time, you may use this knowledge to make your campaigns more effective.

Chapter 2:

Recognising Your Target Market

Any effective marketing effort starts with a thorough understanding of its target market. With your product or service, who are you hoping to reach? What problems and needs do they have? You may modify your marketing messaging in accordance with your target audience after you have a solid grasp of them.

Why is it crucial to comprehend your intended audience?

Knowing who your target audience is is crucial for a variety of reasons.
 Below are a handful:

In order to craft marketing messages that effectively reach your target audience, it is imperative that you have a thorough understanding of them. Your communications will be unfocused and ineffectual.

To pick the appropriate channels for marketing
 Different marketing channels have different qualities. A few networks
make material that is more appropriate for some viewers than for others. You may select the channels where your target audience is most likely to be present by knowing who they are.

To properly distribute your marketing budget:
Since you have a limited budget for marketing, you must be careful with how you use it. You may direct your spending towards the channels and tactics that will yield the best results by having a clear grasp of your target demographic.

A Guide to Recognising Your Target Audience

There's no shortage of approaches to comprehending your target market. Here are some pointers:

Perform market analysis: Market research may be carried out in a variety of methods, including focus groups, interviews, and surveys. Using market research, you may discover more about the characteristics, psychographics, and behaviors of your target audience.

Check your website traffic: Google Analytics is a useful tool for website owners to get information about their website visitors. You may get information from Google Analytics about your visitors' demographics, interests, and behaviors.

Make use of social media listening resources: You can monitor what people are saying on social media about your brand and your industry with the use of social media listening tools. You may use this information to gain a deeper understanding of the requirements and problems of your target audience.

Create a buyer persona: A semi-fictional depiction of your ideal client is called a *buyer persona.* You may gain a deeper understanding of the motives, obstacles, and decision-making process of your target audience by developing buyer personas.

Once you comprehend your goal well
you may begin creating marketing campaigns and
messaging that are specific to their needs.

**The following advice will help you write
persuasive marketing communications for your
intended audience:**

- **Speak to them in their language**:Speak to your intended audience in their native tongue.

- **Focus on their wants and pain points**:Concentrate your marketing communications on how your product or service can solve their issues or enhance their lives.
- Use the terms and phrases that they use.
- **Be particular**: Avoid sweeping generalizations regarding your offering.
- **Use social evidence**: To establish trust with your target audience, use social proof, such as testimonials and customer reviews.
- Be precise about the benefits that it may provide.

By comprehending your intended audience and producing impactful marketing messaging, you may expand your clientele and attract the right clients.

Chapter 3:

Creating a Content Marketing Strategy

The goal of **content marketing,** which is a strategic marketing technique, is to create and disseminate useful, pertinent, and consistent material in order to draw in and hold on to a target audience and encourage lucrative consumer action. A number of long-term company objectives, including raising brand recognition, generating leads, and boosting revenue, may be accomplished with the aid of content marketing.

What is the significance of content marketing?

There are several reasons why content marketing is crucial. Below are a handful:

- **It enables you to engage and attract your target audience:**By producing and disseminating excellent content that speaks to

your target audience, you draw them in and
start a dialogue.
- Building authority and trust is facilitated by
constant production of high-quality

By producing high-quality content, you are gaining
the trust of your target audience and establishing
yourself as an authority in your field.
 It aids in raising your search engine ranks. Superior
content is highly valued by Google and other search
engines. Your website is more likely to rank higher
in search engine results pages (SERPs) when
produce and share high-quality content. This implies
that when people look for terms associated with
your sector, more people will find your website.

- **It facilitates lead generation and sales:**You
establish yourself as a reliable resource when
you produce and disseminate content that
speaks to the needs and pain points of your
target audience. For your company, this may
result in increased leads and revenue.

"How to develop a plan for content marketing

The following procedures must be followed in order to develop an effective content marketing strategy:

1. Explain your objectives:

- **What do you want to accomplish with your content marketing plan?**
- **Which goals are you trying to achieve?**
- **Lead generation, sales, or brand awareness?** You may select the appropriate content subjects and forms once you are aware of your aims.

2. Determine your intended audience:

- **To whom are you attempting to direct your content?**
- **What are their problems and needs?**
- You can produce content that speaks to your target audience if you have a clear understanding of who they are.

3. Assess the content demands of your target audience:

- **What kinds of material are they consuming?**
- **And where do they eat it?**

 Once you are aware of the kind of material You may produce and disseminate content that is specifically catered to the demands of your target audience and the platforms on which they consume it.

4. Generate content ideas: You may begin generating content ideas once you have a clear understanding of the content requirements of your target audience. You may produce a wide range of material, including blog entries, articles, infographics, films, and podcasts.

5. Make a calendar of content: One tool that might help you organize and oversee the production and dissemination of your content is a *content calendar*.

The following details have to be included in a content calendar:
- **Content publication date**
- **Content format**
- **Content topic**
- **Content promotion channels**

6.Produce and disseminate excellent content: After creating a content schedule, you can go to work producing and disseminating excellent content. Make sure must thoroughly revise your work before posting it.

7. Market your product: To ensure that people can find your work, you must market it once it has been published. **Your website, social media accounts**, and **email marketing** may all be used to promote your content.

8. Assess and evaluate your outcomes: To determine what is and is not working with your content marketing initiatives, it is critical to track and evaluate the outcomes. Over time, using this information will enable you to make improvements to your content marketing plan.

The following advice will help you create content marketing initiatives that work:

- **Produce material that speaks to the interests of your intended audience:** Your material has to be pertinent to the requirements and problems of your target audience. Also, it needs to be instructive and captivating.

- **Make use of a range of content formats**: You may produce a wide range of material, including blog entries, articles, infographics, films, and podcasts. Make use of a range of material types to maintain audience interest.
- **Sponsor your content across several platforms**:Don't limit your content promotion to your website. Advertise it on email marketing lists, social media platforms, and other pertinent websites.
- **Remain constant:** Regularly release fresh stuff online. By doing this, you can keep your audience interested and wanting more.

One effective method that might assist you in reaching your company objectives is *content marketing.* With the advice in this chapter, you can develop an effective content marketing plan that will assist you in to increase your search engine ranks, connect with your target audience, establish authority and trust, produce leads, and boost sales.

Chapter 4

Optimizing Your Website for Search Engines

Search engine optimization (SEO) is the process of making your website more search engine friendly so that search engines will list it higher (SERPs). You want your website to show up at the top of the search engine results page (SERP) when prospective buyers look for keywords associated with your product or service.

What makes SEO crucial?

There are several reasons why SEO is significant. Below are a handful:

- **It assists you in connecting with more possible clients**: A better SERP position will draw more visitors to your website. As a result, you will have more chances to expand your clientele and earn money.
- **It facilitates the generation of leads and sales:** Visitors to your website are more likely to convert to leads or customers. Increased leads and sales may result from better-quality website traffic, which SEO may help you with.
- **It provides you with a competitive edge**: In SERPs, several firms are vying for the same keywords. Your website's SEO optimisation might increase the likelihood that it will rank higher than that of your rivals.

Guide to SEO-optimized websites

To optimize your website for search engines, you can take a lot of different steps.
Here are some suggestions:

Make appropriate keyword selections: To begin optimizing your website for search engines, you must *Select the appropriate keywords*. The terms and phrases that consumers are most likely to use while looking for information about your good or service are known as **keywords**. To identify the ideal keywords for your website, employ keyword research tools.

Make sure your meta descriptions and title tags are optimized: The brief passages of text that show up in SERPs are called title tags and meta descriptions. Make careful to optimise them for your goal keywords since they are crucial for SEO.

Produce superior : The material on your website should be educational, of the highest caliber, and pertinent to your target keywords. High-quality content is highly valued by Google and other search engines, so be sure you consistently create it.

Create backlinks: Backlinks are connections to your website made by other websites. A backlink is aare othdata's signal to Google, which may assist you in raising your website's SERP ranking and increasing its visibility in rich snippets.

Although SEO is a challenging and dynamic area, companies of all sizes must use it. You may begin to optimise your website for search engines (SERPs) and raise your website's rating by heeding the advice in this chapter. This may provide you a competitive edge, help you reach more potential clients, and produce leads and sales.

Chapter 5

Using Social Media to Promote Your Product

Social media is an effective instrument that you may use to reach a wide audience while promoting your goods or services. You may begin using social media marketing to reach more prospective clients, produce leads and sales, and cultivate client connections by heeding the advice in this chapter.

With the use of social media, you may effectively reach a wide audience by promoting your goods or services. You may establish direct connections and relationships with potential clients through it.

What makes social media marketing crucial?

There are several reasons why social media marketing is crucial.
Below are a handful:

- **It has a sizable audience**: There are billions of users actively using social media networks. You may reach a sizable group of possible clients by using social media marketing.
- **The goal is:** Based on their demographics, interests, and habits, you may direct your social media marketing messaging towards particular audiences. This implies that you will be able to contact your ideal clients more successfully.
- **This is interactive**: Through social networking, you may have direct conversations with prospective clients.

You may conduct prizes and competitions, reply to their inquiries, and answer their remarks. By doing this, you increase the likelihood that potential clients will become loyal to you and support your business.

- **It costs little**: Marketing on social media is a very cost-effective technique to advertise your goods or services.

The majority of social networking sites include both paid and free advertising choices.

How to advertise your goods on social media

Social media may be used in a variety of ways to market your goods. Here are some pointers:

- **Select appropriate social media networks**: Social media networks are not made equally by particular companies and product kinds are more suited for particular social media networks than others. Look into which social networking sites are the most popular and ideal for your company.
- **Produce excellent content:**Similar to content marketing, you must provide top-notch material that speaks to and meets the demands and pain areas of your target audience. Blog entries, articles, infographics, films, and podcasts may all fall under this category.
- **Use social media to promote your content**: After producing top-notch content, you must share it on social media. Post material on your social media profiles and invite your followers to do the same.

- **Hold freebies and competitions on social media**: Giveaways and competitions on social media are excellent methods to interact with your fans and market your goods. Make sure the gifts you are offering will appeal to your fans.

Make use of social media marketing Social media marketing is excellent to expand your audience and tailor your advertisements at particular demographics. The majority of social media networks let you select the kind of advertising that best suits your objectives and financial constraints.

The following are some more pointers for using social media to advertise your product:

- **Stay consistent:** Share content on social media often to maintain your fans' attention.
- **Make use of pertinent hashtags: Adding hashtags(#)** to your content is an excellent approach to increase its visibility. For social media posts, make sure your hashtags are relevant.
- **Participate in conversations with your followers**: Answer their queries and remarks.

This demonstrates your want to establish a rapport with them.

- **Apply social media analytics**:The majority of social networking sites have analytics tools that enable them.

You monitor how well your social media marketing campaigns are working. Utilize these resources to determine what is and is not effective so that you may gradually enhance your efforts.

Chapter 6

Using Paid Advertising to Promote Your Product

Using paid advertising is a terrific method to advertise your goods or services faster and to reach a larger audience. There are several paid advertising networks accessible, including Amazon Ads, LinkedIn Ads, Facebook Ads, and Google Ads.

Why is it vital to use sponsored advertising?"

Paying for advertising is crucial for several reasons. These are very helpful:

- **A wide audience is reached by it**:Through paid advertising channels, you may connect with a lot of prospective clients. If you're attempting to break into a new market or are new to company, this is really beneficial.
- **The aim is**:Based on their demographics, interests, and actions, you may target particular groups of individuals with your sponsored advertising messages. This implies

that you may more successfully contact your desired clientele.

- **It can be measured**: Platforms for paid advertising offer thorough analytics so you can monitor the effectiveness of your campaigns. With this data, you can maximise your budget and make gradual improvements to your ads.
- **It's reasonably priced**: Paid advertising is often quite inexpensive, especially when contrasted with more conventional forms of advertising. You control the spending and just have to pay when someone clicks on your advertisement.

How to market your goods using sponsored advertising

You may market your goods through paid advertising in a variety of ways. Here are some pointers:

- **Select the appropriate platform for sponsored advertising:** Paid advertising networks are not made equal to specific businesses and goods are more appropriate for specific paid advertising platforms than others. Choose the paid advertising platform that will work best for your business by doing some research.

- **Assign objectives:** With your sponsored advertising initiatives, what goals do you want to accomplish? Which goals are you trying to achieve? Lead generation, sales, or brand awareness? You may select the best targeting choices and bidding techniques if you are aware of your objectives.

- **Make excellent advertisements:** You should write compelling and well-researched commercials. They should also speak to the wants and problems of your target audience and be pertinent to them.
- **Assign a budget**: Prior to launching your sponsored advertising efforts, decide on your budget. This will assist you in keeping tabs on your expenditures and ensuring that you are optimising your financial plan.

- **Monitor your outcomes**: It is crucial to monitor the outcomes of your sponsored marketing initiatives so that you may determine what is and is not effective. You may maximise your money and make gradual improvements to your campaigns with the use of this information.

These are some more pointers for promoting your goods with paid advertising:

- **Employ negative keywords:** Negative keywords stop your adverts from appearing for pointless searches. By doing this, you may increase marketing performance and save money.

- **Ad extensions should be used**: Ad extensions include more details about your company, including contact details like your address, phone number, and website links. This might improve the relevance and information in your adverts, increasing clickthrough rates and conversion rates.

- **Try these several ad variations:** Examine several ad versions, including

- **Test various ad version**s: Experiment with several ad variations, including headers, descriptions, and pictures. This will assist you in identifying the ad versions that resonate most with your target market.

Employ remarketing Remarketing enables you to display your adverts to website visitors who have already come to your site. This is a terrific method to remind customers about your company and entice them to return and finish their transaction.

Afterthought

With the help of paid advertising, you can rapidly and effectively promote your goods or services to a larger audience. With the help of this chapter's advice, you may begin utilising paid advertising to expand your client base, improve leads and sales, and expand your company.

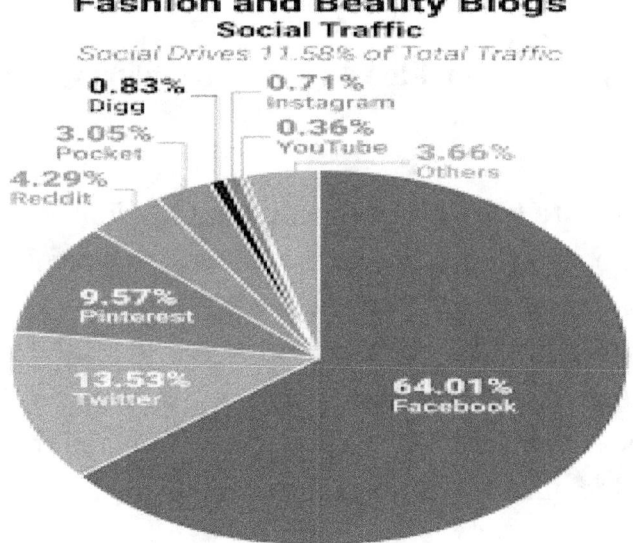

Fashion and Beauty Blogs
Social Traffic
Social Drives 11.58% of Total Traffic

- **0.83%** Digg
- **0.71%** Instagram
- **3.05%** Pocket
- **0.36%** YouTube
- **3.66%** Others
- **4.29%** Reddit
- **9.57%** Pinterest
- **13.53%** Twitter
- **64.01%** Facebook

Chapter 7

Evaluating the Outcomes of Your Internet Marketing Activities

It's critical to track the outcomes of your internet marketing campaigns in order to determine what is and is not effective. With this data, you can maximise your budget and make gradual improvements to your ads.

You may monitor a wide range of parameters, including:

- **Website traffic**:The quantity of individuals who visit your website may serve as a useful gauge for the effectiveness of your internet marketing campaigns.
- **Leads generated**:An excellent measure of the success of your web marketing operations is the quantity of leads they produce.

- **Sales**: The most crucial measure to monitor is the quantity of sales brought about by your internet marketing initiatives, since it gauges how your efforts will affect your bottom line.

You may measure customized metrics for each of your online marketing channels in addition to these broad analytics.For instance, you may monitor the following data for your initiatives including search engine optimisation (SEO):

- **Organic traffic:**The quantity of people that find your website through natural search results.
- **Keyword rankings**:** How your website appears in search engine results for pertinent keywords (SERPs).
- **Backlinks**: The quantity of links pointing to your website from other websites.

In addition to these general metrics, you can also track specific metrics for each of your online marketing channels. For example, you can track the following metrics for your search engine optimization (SEO) campaigns:

- **Organic traffic**:The number of visitors to your website who come from organic search results.
- **Keyword rankings**:The position of your website in search engine results pages (SERPs) for relevant keywords.
- **Backlinks**:The number of links from other websites to your website.

For your social media marketing campaigns, you can track the following metrics:

- **Reach**:The number of people who see your social media posts.
- **Engagement**: The number of people who like, comment, or share your social media posts.
- **Click-through rate (CTR)**:The percentage of people who click on your social media posts.

For your paid advertising campaigns, you can track the following metrics:

- **Impressions**: The number of times your ad is shown.
- **Clicks**: The number of times your ad is clicked.
- **Cost per click (CPC):**The average amount you pay each time someone clicks on your ad.
- **Conversion rate:**The percentage of people who click on your ad and then take a desired action, such as making a purchase or signing up for your email list.

You can use a variety of tools to track the results of your online marketing efforts.
Google Analytics is a free tool that can be used to track website traffic, leads generated, and sales. Social media analytics tools, such as Facebook Insights and Twitter Analytics, can be used to track social media engagement and reach. Paid advertising platforms, such as Google Ads, Amazon Ads and Facebook Ads, provide detailed analytics that can be

used to track the performance of your paid advertising campaigns.

Once you have tracked the results of your online marketing efforts, you can start to analyze them. Look for trends and patterns to see what is working well and what is not. Use this information to improve your campaigns over time and get the most out of your budget.

Here are a few tips for measuring the results of your online marketing efforts:

- **Set clear goals for each of your online marketing campaigns.**This will help you to determine which metrics to track and how to analyze your results.
- **Use a variety of tools to track your results.**This will give you a complete picture of the performance of your online marketing efforts.
- **Analyze your results regularly.**Look for trends and patterns to see what is working well and what is not.

- **Use your findings to improve your campaigns over time**.

This will help you to get the most out of your budget and achieve your online marketing goals.

Measuring the results of your online marketing efforts is essential for improving your campaigns over time and getting the most out of your budget. By tracking the right metrics and analyzing your results regularly, you can identify what is working well and what is not. This information can then be used to improve your campaigns and achieve your online marketing goals

CONCLUSION

In today's competitive market, it is more important than ever to have a strong online presence. By following the tips in this book, you can create and implement a successful online marketing strategy that will help you reach your target audience and grow your business.

Here are a few key takeaways from this book:

- **Define your goals:***What do you want to achieve with your online marketing efforts?*
- **Understand your target audience:***Who are you trying to reach with your product or service?*
- **Create high-quality content:** Content marketing is a great way to attract and engage potential customers.
- **Optimize your website for search engines**: This will help people find your website when they search for keywords related to your product or service.

- **Use social media to promote your product or service:**Social media is a powerful tool that can help you reach a large audience.
- **Measure your results:**It is important to track the results of your online marketing efforts so that you can see what is working and what is not.

Here are five best marketing tools that you can use to market your product online:

1. Google Analytics: Google Analytics is a free web analytics service that provides insights into your website traffic and user behavior. It can help you track your website's performance, identify areas for improvement, and understand your audience better.

2. Google Ads: Google Ads is an online advertising platform that allows you to create and run ads on Google Search, YouTube, and other Google properties. It can be a powerful tool for reaching your target audience and driving traffic to your website.

3. **Canva**:Canva is a graphic design platform that makes it easy to create professional-looking graphics without any design experience. It can be used to create social media graphics, blog posts, presentations, and more.

4. **HubSpot:** HubSpot is a marketing, sales, and service **CRM** platform that helps businesses attract, engage, and delight their customers. It offers a wide range of tools for marketing automation, email marketing, social media management, and more.

5. **MailChimp**: MailChimp is an email marketing platform that makes it easy to create and send email newsletters. It offers a variety of features for creating targeted email campaigns, tracking email performance, and managing your email list.

In addition to these five powerful tools, there are many other marketing tools and strategies that you can use to market your product online.

Some additional tools to consider include:

Social media: Social media can be a great way to connect with your target audience and promote your product. Use platforms like **Facebook**, **Twitter**, **Instagram**, and **LinkedIn** to share content, interact with followers, and run ads.

Content marketing: Content marketing involves creating and sharing valuable, relevant, and consistent content to attract and retain a clearly defined audience — and, ultimately, to drive profitable customer action. Use content marketing to create blog posts, articles, infographics, and videos that will educate and inform your potential customers about your product.

SEO (search engine optimisation): Increasing your website's search engine ranking through optimisation is known as **search engine optimisation (SEO) (SERPs).** This can help you attract more organic traffic to your website and increase your sales.

Influencer marketing: Influencer marketing involves partnering with influencers in your industry to promote your product. Influencers are people who have a large following on social media or other online platforms. They can help you reach a wider audience and build credibility for your product.

Pay-per-click (PPC) advertising:*PPC advertising is a form of online advertising where you pay each time someone clicks on your ad. This can be a great way to drive traffic to your website and generate leads.

**The best marketing tools and strategies for your business will depend on your specific product, target audience, and budget. **

By following these tips, you can create and implement a successful online marketing strategy that will help you reach your target audience and grow your business.

Remember, **online marketing** is a journey, not a destination.Results need to be seen with patience, persistence, and time.But if you are committed to success, you will eventually achieve your goals.

So what are you waiting for? Start today and create a successful online marketing strategy for your business!